THE FASCINATING WORLD OF...

BEES

by

Angels Julivert

Illustrations by Carlos de Miguel

BARRON'S

THE BEE: A SOCIAL INSECT

Bees, along with wasps and ants, belong to the order *hymenoptera*. Their small, hairy bodies are divided into three parts: **head**, **thorax**, and **abdomen**.

Bees are aware of what goes on around them through sense organs in their heads and legs.

They see movements, direct their flight, and distinguish the colors of flowers through their enormous compound eyes, which are composed of thousands of tiny units called **facets**.

The senses of hearing, smell, and touch are located in their antennae and legs, and are essential when the bees are in the darkness of the hive. They can recognize their comrades and detect enemies through their sense of smell.

Bees are social insects. This means that they live in a community in which each bee carries out a specific function that is absolutely necessary for the survival of the colony.

There are three types of bees in a hive: one **queen**, thousands of industrious **worker bees**, and hundreds of chubby, lazy **drones**.

Right: Bees are perfect social insects, although if we look at the hive's appearance, all we see is a great many bees moving in a disorderly fashion. This book is an exciting journey into this fascinating world.

THE HEAD OF THE BEE, FRONTAL VIEW

EYES

ANTENNA

UPPER JAW

TONGUE

■ **THE HEAD:** two large eyes, a pair of antennae, and the mouth.

■ **THE THORAX:** two pairs of wings and three pairs of legs.

■ **THE ABDOMEN:** the queen and the workers have a sting.

BEES CHANGE THEIR BODIES

During its life cycle, the bee passes through four very different phases:

- Egg
- Larva
- Pupa
- Adult

Like the butterfly, the bee goes through a **metamorphosis**. The larva is very different from the adult and during its development, the bee's body goes through important changes.

Would you like to follow the process?

The queen lays an **egg** in a small cavity called a cell. All of the eggs look the same, but there are two types: fertilized eggs, which become females, and unfertilized eggs, which will turn into males.

After three days, the **larva** hatches. It does not have wings or legs but looks like a small worm. The larva eats a lot and grows rapidly. Within a short time, it occupies the entire cell.

At this time, it enters the phase of the **pupa** and the workers seal the entrance to the cell. There, hidden away, an incredible transformation begins: little by little, the pupa changes its form, developing wings and legs.

Once the metamorphosis is finished, the **adult** bee emerges, completely formed.

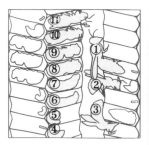

Right: The metamorphosis occurs in the sealed brood cells. ① The queen lays an egg. ② A worker sucks up honey. ③ Another worker feeds a larva. ④ to ⑦ Larva. ⑧ and ⑨ Developing pupae. ⑩ and ⑪ Adult bees beginning to break open their cells to come out.

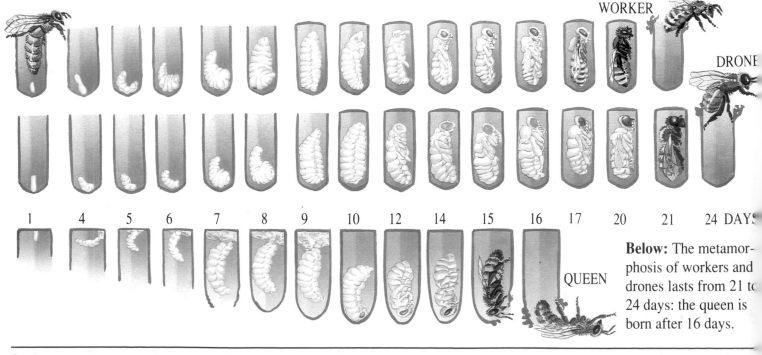

WORKER

DRONE

QUEEN

| 1 | 4 | 5 | 6 | 7 | 8 | 9 | 10 | 12 | 14 | 15 | 16 | 17 | 20 | 21 | 24 DAYS |

Below: The metamorphosis of workers and drones lasts from 21 to 24 days: the queen is born after 16 days.

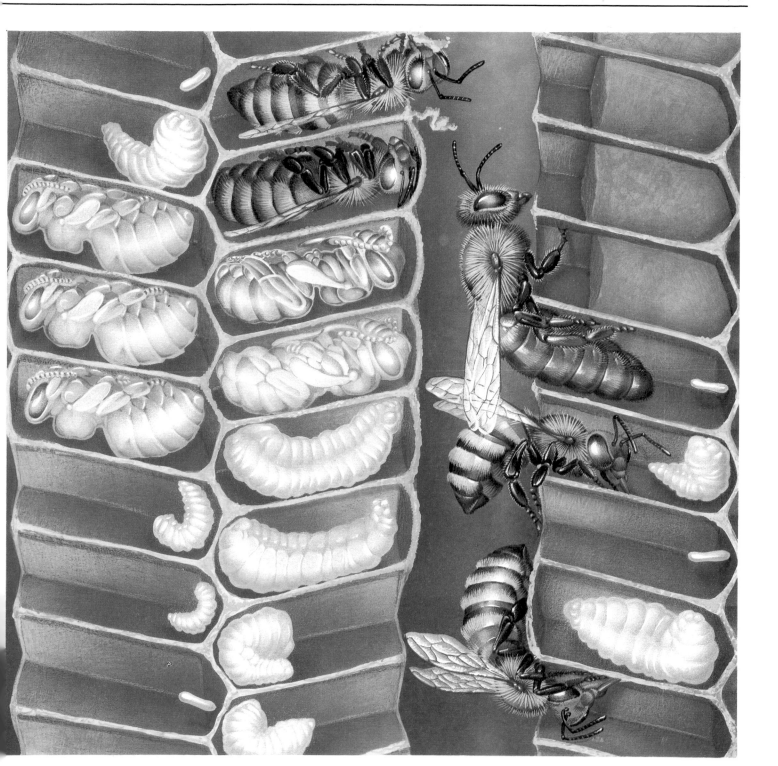

THE IDEAL COUPLE: THE QUEEN AND THE DRONE

There is only one queen in each colony and she is the only female capable of laying eggs.

The queen never leaves the hive, and during her entire life, which may last from three to five years, she dedicates herself exclusively to the laying of eggs.

The queen is born of a fertilized egg and during her growth the workers give her a special food called **royal jelly**.

You can tell her from the rest of the inhabitants of the hive by her size: She is the largest, has a longer abdomen, and her sting is smooth and curved.

In contrast to the workers, she does not attack people or animals, and only uses her sting against other queens. She may lay up to 2,000 eggs a day, although this depends on each queen and also on her age.

The males, or drones, do no work. The are incapable of feeding themselves and have no sting. Their most spectacular feature is their enormous eyes, formed by a much larger number of facets than those of the workers or the queen. They live only about three months and their only function is to mate with young queens.

Right: The queen is always surrounded by workers, who never stop touching her with their antennae, through which they receive certain chemicals called **pheromones**. The workers also touch each other. By this process the energy of the queen is transmitted throughout the hive.

Left: It may be that all bees look alike to you. Nevertheless, it is not difficult to see the differences between the **queen**, who is the largest and has a long, slim abdomen; the **workers**, who are the smallest; and the **drones**, who have a shorter, stubbier abdomen than the queen.

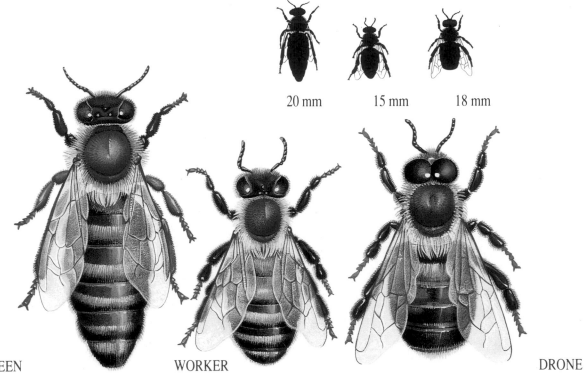

20 mm   15 mm   18 mm

QUEEN   WORKER   DRONE

THE WORKERS, AT THE SERVICE OF THE QUEEN

O f the three types of bees that live in the hive, the most numerous are the workers. They are all **sterile females**, which means that they cannot lay eggs. Like the queen, they are born of fertilized eggs, but they receive a different type of food as larvae, and for this reason develop in a different manner.

The worker bees take charge of all the work to be done and their lives are very short. In spring and summer, the period of greatest activity, they live only four to five weeks. In winter, when there is less to be done, they may live several months.

Workers have a sort of "basket" on each hind leg, which they use to transport the pollen they gather from flowers. They are also responsible for making the honeybee's delicious honey, and for feeding the queen, her offspring, and the males. They also produce beeswax, which they use to build honeycombs.

With their straight, barbed stings, they sting anything that tries to bother them or make its way into the hive, but they would never attack a queen. As you can see, the workers perform a very important role.

WORKER
SECRETING
WAX

WAX
GLANDS

WAX
PLATES

HIND LEG OF
A WORKER

CLOSE-UP OF
POLLEN BASKET

POLLEN
BALLS

POLLEN BASKET

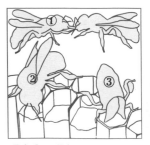

Right: The workers manufacture honey from the nectar of flowers, which they pass from one to another ①. They also fill and inspect the storage cells ② and ③.

Left: The workers are also the only ones that secrete beeswax for the construction of honeycombs, through glands called **wax glands.**

Left: On their hind legs the workers have a cavity called the **pollen basket.** This is where they accumulate the pollen they collect from flowers.

DIVISION OF LABOR

Within the hive, the jobs to be done are perfectly organized. Each worker performs a task according to her age, meaning that she changes occupations through the course of her life:

■ As soon as they are born, workers serve as **house bees,** cleaning the empty cells so that they can be used again.

■ **Nurse bees** are three to ten days old and they care for and feed the brood. They make a special food necessary for the development of the larvae.

■ Later on, their job is to build new cells and repair the old ones. Now **wax bees,** they always have plenty to do.

■ After a few more days, they begin to store the nectar and pollen brought in by their comrades to be used as reserves in the winter.

■ **Guard bees** are entrusted with the defense of the hive. With their antennae, they inspect anyone trying to enter.

■ The **foragers** are the oldest and most expert bees. They are more than three weeks old. Thus, they are given the most difficult task: that of gathering pollen and nectar. These are the bees that you see flying from flower to flower.

Right: The activity of the workers is unending. Here we see workers engaged in the following activities: ① Attending the queen; ② cleaning out the pollen in their pollen baskets; ③ a guard bee dragging a drone; ④ wax bees contructing a comb; ⑤ a nurse bee feeding a larva; ⑥ a house bee cleaning a comb of leftover wax; ⑦ bees fanning honey with their wings; ⑧ a forager bee filling a cell with honey.

Below: Foragers returning to their hive. Their pollen baskets are full of pollen and their throats are full of nectar.

FULL POLLEN BASKET

THE NUPTIAL FLIGHT AND THE DEATH OF THE DRONES

Right: In each hive, half a dozen queen larvae are nursed. The first to emerge goes through the cells and kills her rivals. If she finds one out of its cell, the two fight to the death. Whichever is victorious will be the new queen of the colony.

Left: Previously, the old queen has abandoned the hive, followed by many workers and a few drones. They rest on the branch of a tree, forming a thick bunch of bees called a swarm.

Toward the end of spring, the drones are born and so are the future queens. It is at this time of year that a change of queen comes about.

The old queen leaves the hive, accompanied by a group of workers, and lights on the branch of a tree. Her companions unite around her in a thick bunch; a swarm has formed.

Shortly after the old queen's departure, the first young queen is born, and goes through the hive looking for her rivals, whom she kills while they are still defenseless in their cells. If any rival is already out of the cell, the two confront each other in a battle to the death.

The victor commences her nuptial flight. She flies very high and the drones follow her, attracted by her odor. The male mates with her in the air and, as he tries to separate himself from her, his abdomen bursts open and he dies. The queen returns to the hive.

The rest of the drones live for a while at the expense of the colony. They now serve no purpose. When winter draws near and food becomes scarce, the workers expel them from the hive and do not hesitate to attack them if they try to reenter. The males, incapable of feeding themselves, soon die.

NUPTIAL FLIGHT

Above: During the nuptial flight, the new queen leaves the hive, followed by several drones. The queen is fertilized by a few drones, who die when they try to separate themselves from her.

THE HIVE, A LABYRINTH OF CELLS

The hive is composed of various combs, which are parallel sheets of wax with a small passageway between them where the bees can move about.

Each comb is formed of numerous cells, small six-sided (**hexagonal**) chambers where the bees store food (pollen and honey) and lodge the brood (larvae and pupae). They are tilted slightly so that their contents cannot fall out.

The brood cells are not found in all the combs, nor are they all alike: The royal cells are the largest. They are tube-shaped and are destined for future queens, while the brood cells for workers are hexagonal and are the most numerous. Those that contain future drones are somewhat larger than those for workers.

It is fascinating to watch how bees construct their combs. They hang from one another by their legs and begin to secrete small flakes of wax which they chew with their jaws. Later they put the wax in place and mold it until the comb is completed (from top to bottom).

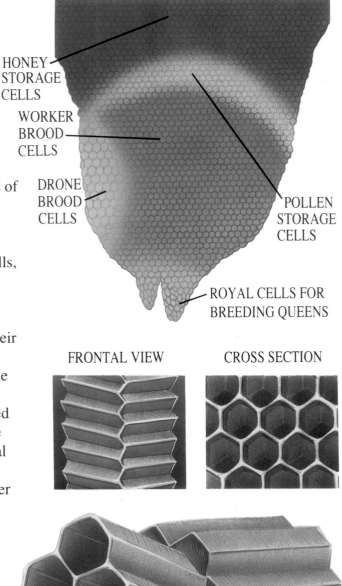

HONEY STORAGE CELLS

WORKER BROOD CELLS

DRONE BROOD CELLS

POLLEN STORAGE CELLS

ROYAL CELLS FOR BREEDING QUEENS

FRONTAL VIEW

CROSS SECTION

SECTION OF A PORTION OF COMB

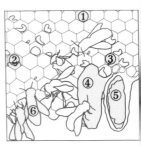

Right: Here you can see the cells of the comb better, including: ① storage cells; ② drone brood cells; ③ worker brood cells; ④ and ⑤ a sealed royal cell and a cross section of another royal cell with the pupa of a queen; ⑥ workers constructing the comb.

Left: The cells are slightly tilted to prevent the honey or pollen from spilling.

INTRUDERS IN THE HIVE

There are many creatures that like the bees' honey: **bears**, who destroy hives, and insects such as **wasps, ants,** or **beetles** that sneak in to rob the bees of their sweet food.

The **hawkmoth** is an insect that slips into the hive and with its long snout sucks up stored honey.

Bees also have to watch out for the caterpillars of certain moths which eat beeswax, destroying their combs.

The guard bees are responsible for chasing away intruders by attacking them with their stings.

WORKER COLLECTING PROPOLIS

Right: The hawkmoth is an insect that steals honey. The bees attack it and then drag it outside ①. Other visitors are beetles ②. One bee raises its abdomen and discharges a fragrant substance that warns the rest of the bees ③.

Left: Propolis is a substance that bees collect from the bark of trees. It is used to cover intruders that are trapped in the hive.

ENLARGEMENT OF A STING

Right: The queen and the workers have stings with which they inject poison. When they smell danger, the guard workers go into a state of alert, raising their heads and thoraxes and lowering their abdomens.

WORKER IN STATE OF ALERT

When an animal or an insect dies inside the hive, the workers drag it out. But if the corpse is too heavy for them, they cover it with a substance called **propolis** which contains resins from the bark of certain trees. Propolis keeps the corpse from rotting

When a bee stings another insect, the bee is unharmed. Then why does she die when she attacks a human? The skin of mammals is more resistant and the sting, which is barbed, acts like a harpoon. When the bee tries to pull it out, her abdomen rips open and she dies.

PROBLEMS IN THE HIVE

Apart from their numerous enemies, other dangers may await the bees and threaten their survival.

■ Sometimes a colony loses its queen. In that case, the workers feed a larva that is less than three days old the special diet of royal jelly. They also enlarge its cell so that it has room to develop as a new queen.

■ Although bees are protected within the hive, too much cold or heat could cause the death of the entire colony.

In order to survive, bees need to maintain the proper temperature inside the hive. How do they do it?

In winter they form a tightly knit group around the queen and "shiver," making their muscles contract and expand very rapidly. This raises the temperature. On the other hand, in summer they move their little wings, making an air current that cools them.

Even more dangerous to the colony are disease-causing parasites such as the mite. This tiny creature lives on top of the bees, either as larva, pupa, or adult, and feeds off their internal juices, weakening them little by little.

95° F (35° C)

86° F (30° C)

59° F (15° C)

48° F (9° C)

Right: In summer, bees fight the heat by moving their wings, producing a current that cools the hive. On the hottest days, bees cool down the hive by carrying in water.

Left: On the most severe days of winter, the bees pack together around the queen, leaving a few paths open so that air can circulate: In the central area, the temperature is 95° Fahrenheit (35° C). On the outer edges, it is much cooler. There is a constant movement of bees from the exterior to the center.

THE DANCE OF THE BEES

The most curious and fascinating way in which bees communicate among themselves is the so-called **dance of the bees**. They use this "language" to transmit any important discovery, such as, for example, where to find lots of nectar or a good place to construct a hive.

The movements of the scout bee when she "dances" indicate to her comrades the distance and also the direction in which to go.

The speed of the dance signals the abundance of the food source.

Bees perform two types of dances:

■ The **circular dance** tells the bees that they should look close to the hive—within 300 feet (100 m). The scout bee begins to trace circles on top of a comb, sometimes turning to the left and other times to the right. She repeats the dance several times while the other workers follow her and touch her with their antennae.

■ The **wag-tail dance** signifies that the place is far off—more than 300 feet (100 m) away. The bee traces a figure eight on top of the comb.

First she walks in a straight line, wagging her abdomen. Then she traces half a circle on either side.

The straight line indicates the direction, and the number of repetitions of the entire figure indicates the distance.

Right: The wag-tail section of the dance signals the direction of the discovery.

Below: With the circular dance, the scout bee lets her comrades know that her discovery was made close to the hive.

Right: Scout bees perform the wag-tail dance for their comrades to communicate the location of a distant supply of nectar or pollen.

CIRCULAR DANCE

BEES AND POLLINATION

Pollination is the transport of pollen from the stamens of one flower to the stigma of another, producing the seeds which will make a new plant.

In some cases, pollen is transported by the wind, but there are plants that depend on animals and, especially, insects, to achieve pollination.

Bees are one of the most important pollinating insects, since they visit many flowers. When they alight on a flower, their bodies become covered with pollen and, on visiting the next flower, a part of this pollen falls off, pollinating the plant.

Bees are very important in agriculture. Many of the plants we cultivate, especially fruit trees (pears, apples, plums, etc.), depend on insects for their pollination.

Hives are sometimes installed close to cultivated plants to improve pollination and thus obtain a richer and more abundant harvest.

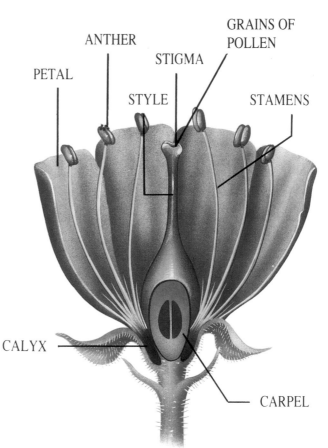

PETAL
ANTHER
STIGMA
GRAINS OF POLLEN
STYLE
STAMENS
CALYX
CARPEL

Right: Bees suck up nectar with their proboscis and transport it to their hives in their honey crops; with it they make honey. They also collect pollen in the pollen baskets on their hind legs. But bees are also very important to flowers, because thanks to the pollen they transport on their legs, some plants are fertilized.

Right: When a bee alights on a flower, her body becomes covered with pollen. Some of it falls off during flight and makes possible the development of seeds and the birth of new flowers.

PRODUCERS OF HONEY

Bees are insects that have a "sweet tooth." Their daily foods are pollen and honey.

The foragers gather **pollen**, which they store in little balls in the pollen baskets on their legs. They also gather the nectar of flowers.

The queen and the drones are unable to find food for themselves. They are fed by the workers, who also feed the brood.

The nurse bees secrete a very nutritious food, royal jelly, with which they nourish the queens during their entire development. On the other hand, the worker and drone larvae receive a mixture of pollen and honey.

How do honeybees produce their honey? The transformation of nectar to honey begins when the forager bee transports the nectar in her honey crop. Once in the hive, it is passed from one worker to another. The nectar mixes with saliva, loses water, and changes into honey.

At that point the workers store it in cells. Since it is still quite liquid, the workers fan it with their wings. This causes some of the water to evaporate.

When the honey has ripened, the cells are sealed with wax to prevent it from spoiling.

Below: Stamens are thin filaments that emerge from the calyx of a flower and become thicker at their ends, which is where the pollen accumulates. The forager bee fills its pollen baskets with pollen. Nectar is sucked up through the bee's proboscis.

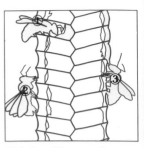

Right: The workers pass the recently gathered nectar among themselves. Mixed with saliva, it loses water and turns to honey. Later, they deposit it in storage cells ①. For several days they fan the cells so that the honey thickens ②. When it is ripe, they seal the cells with wax ③.

BEEKEEPING

Beekeeping consists of the care and breeding of bees in order to obtain their products: the person who does this is called a **beekeeper**.

The artificial hives that humans offer bees are quite varied and have evolved over time. The most old-fashioned are simple hollow trunks or wicker baskets. Today, beekeepers use different types of boxes that are much more practical and manageable.

The beekeeper knows the best moment to harvest the honey and how much can be extracted without harming the bees. The beekeeper takes out only the combs that contain ripe honey and puts them in a centrifuge. This machine extracts the honey without breaking the honeycombs, which can be used again. Before putting the honey in jars, the beekeeper filters it so that any pieces of wax are removed.

Honey is also used in the manufacture of other products, such as candies and jams. In addition, we obtain many other products from bees, such as **beeswax**, **pollen**, and **royal jelly**.

Right: During bees' handling, the beekeeper is clothed protectively ① and is helped by a smoke-blower ②, which stupefies the bees.

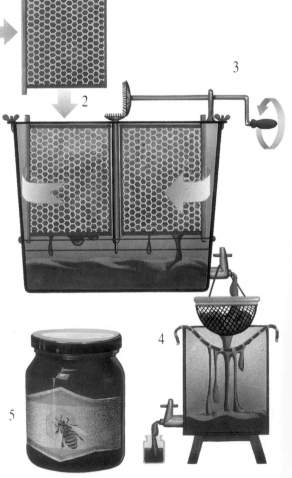

Below: Beekeeping has been practiced for many years. In former times barrels and baskets were used as hives.

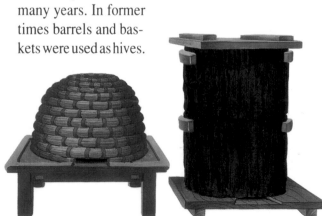

Above and Right: The honeycomb is removed from the artificial hive (1); it is put into a centrifuge (2) which, rotating at very high speed (3), extracts the honey; the honey drops into a collecting tank (4) and is later filtered and packed into jars (5).

Glossary

abdomen. The back part of the body behind the thorax.

antenna. The organ of sensation located on the bee's head.

apiculture. Keeping bees to obtain various products made by them, such as honey, wax, royal jelly, etc.

calyx. The outer leafy part of a flower.

combs. Parallel sheets of wax with a small passageway between them where the bees move about.

compound eye. Type of insect eye, which is generally large and found in pairs. It is formed by units or facets, each of which functions as an independent eye. A bee's vision, and that of all insects, is like a mosaic composed of the many images viewed through each different sector or facet.

drone. The male bee; it has no sting and does not gather honey.

facets. Tiny units that make up the compound eyes of the bee.

foragers. The oldest and most expert bees; they gather pollen and nectar.

guard bees. Bees that defend the hive.

hawkmoth. An insect that uses its long proboscis to suck up stored honey from the hive.

Hymenoptera. An order of insects, which includes bees, wasps, and ants.

larva. Stage of bee development. The larva hatches from an egg and has no wings or legs.

metamorphosis. Transformation that occurs in the body of a bee, during its development.

nuptial flight. Flight a queen bee and various drones make out of the hive, during which the queen is fertilized.

nurse bees. Bees that are three to ten days old who care for and feed the larvae.

pheromones. Chemicals produced by the queen bee and received through their antennae by the workers.

pollen basket. A cavity, located on their hind legs, in which the workers accumulate the pollen they collect from flowers.

pollination. Transporting pollen from the stamen of one flower to the female parts of another, thus achieving reproduction of the plant.

proboscis. The organ with which insects suck up nectar.

propolis. A substance containing resins from the bark of certain trees, wax, etc.; it keeps a corpse that has died inside the hive from rotting.

pupa. Stage of bee development, immediately following the larval phase, during which the wings and legs begin to form.

royal jelly. Food made by worker bees out of pollen, honey, and various vitamins. The wet-nurse workers feed the royal jelly to all larvae, without exception, during their first three days of life. After the third day, they reserve the royal jelly for those larvae destined to be queens.

social insect. Insects that live in colonies and form a perfectly ordered society in which tasks are divided among all members. Bees, ants, and certain wasps are social insects.

stamen. A thin, pollen-bearing filament within the calyx of a flower.

swarm. A number of bees grouped together outside of the hive.

thorax. The body of the bee containing two pairs of wings and three pairs of legs.

wax glands. Glands through which beeswax for the construction of honeycombs is secreted by the workers.

Index

Boldface numbers indicate illustrations